# You Write,
# They Pay

### *How to Build a Thriving Writing Business from NOTHING!*

By: Susan Anderson

www.workingwriterhappywriter.com

Published by ✒ Archangel Ink

ISBN: 1942761376
ISBN-13: 978-1-942761-37-2

# Disclaimer

Although the author and publisher have made every effort to ensure that the information in this book was correct at press time, the author and publisher do not assume and hereby disclaim any liability to any party for any loss, damage, or disruption caused by errors or omissions, whether such errors or omissions result from negligence, accident, or any other cause.

The freelance writing business is not for everyone. Income results are based on a variety of factors; therefore, we have no way of knowing how well you will do. Your background, your work habits, business skills, and further personal skills will determine how well you do in any business you undertake. Therefore, we do not guarantee that you will get rich, do well, or make any money at all. In reading this book and putting the contents to use, you accept full responsibility for your own results.

*For the joy of the journey and the pleasurable accompaniment of other creators.*

*To God be the glory—great things He has done.*

# Foreword

The curse of knowledge.

That's the in-vogue term used to describe an expert's inability to think about a problem from the perspective of a novice.

I was that novice back in 2003, the year I decided to launch my part-time freelance writing business.

As I researched ideas and options, it was clear that much of the advice I came across was geared toward established freelancers. And when I *did* come across material for beginners, the content often felt outdated, incomplete, or irrelevant for my situation.

It was frustrating, to say the least!

Even today, it's challenging to find practical advice on how to get started as a freelance writer—advice that's grounded in reality, is based on the current outsourcing landscape, and is focused on the best available success paths.

That's what I love about *You Write, They Pay*. In this book, Susan Anderson details what's actually working today in the world of freelance writing. It's based on reality, not some theoretical or outdated scenario. And her advice is clear, sound, and simple, which makes it easier to consume and implement.

I also respect the fact that Susan has "been there, done that." She endured enough struggle as a budding freelancer to remember what it was like to start from scratch—the mistakes, self-doubt, confusion, and fear. The fact that she still works closely with new writers keeps her grounded and in touch with her readers.

And as you'll soon discover, Susan is a great teacher. She's done a masterful job of taking a big, complex topic and distilling it into actionable steps anyone can follow. And she's done it with a friendly and encouraging tone (and a good dose of humor!).

Study this material. But above all, apply it diligently. It will work if you work it.

Ed Gandia
Co-author, *The Wealthy Freelancer*
Host, *High-Income Business Writing* podcast
www.b2blauncher.com

# Table of Contents

# Is This You?

The final straw was being told what time I could take a bathroom break.

I'd just taken a temp job at a nonprofit organization, and my supervisor was laying out the rules.

That was it.

With a college degree, half a Master's, and a long history of being a stellar employee—but always wishing I could find a career that really fit—being told I could only "go" when I had permission gave me the courage I needed to make a change.

Maybe you're in the same place.

You might be working at a job that's okay, but really not what you ever dreamed about. Maybe it's not even okay, and you'd leave in a heartbeat if you could find another way to make money. Maybe you have children at home and want to find something you can do that doesn't completely disrupt your family life—you want to work just a little when they're at school or napping. Maybe you're dying to go travel the world and want a business you can do from anywhere. Maybe you're retired and want to try your hand at something new or make some extra money—and the idea of being a greeter at Walmart doesn't do it for you.

If any of these scenarios sound familiar, then this book is for you!

There's a whole world of writing out there that you may have never considered. It's easy to get jobs that pay well. It's never boring. You can be picky about what you'll write about and whom you'll write for. And you can do it anywhere you've got a computer. In fact, I've worked from all over the United States, in Guatemala, and even in Fiji!

If you want to start a writing business of your own, you could definitely go the route of hiring a coach. That's what I did—to the tune of $5,000 back in 2005. Best money I ever spent—so much so that I've hired several coaches since. A good coach's input and guidance flattens the learning curve and nudges you forward toward your dreams.

But if you're not in a position to lay out that kind of cash, this book may be a pretty good substitute to get you started.

**First, a confession: I can't teach you how to write.**

I can teach you how to write many of the projects that businesses will hire you to write. I can teach you how to build a business. I can even teach you how to build an agency of writers to ramp up your earning capacity.

I can teach those skills because I remember learning them. Not so with writing. It's always come naturally to me. So, I can't teach you that—you've got to have some talent coming into this.

But the rest? Game on!

There are so many topics we could cover here, but my goal in this book is to help you see what's possible and how to earn your first dollars as a freelance business writer. We'll take it from there in other books and in my Bootcamp course. (OK, I felt your impatience there—I'll give you details on that at the end of the book. Now you're probably flipping to the end... it's okay, we'll wait.)

This book will answer the questions buzzing around in your brain:

- What IS this business? Is it real? You mean to tell me that people will pay me to write for them?
- They say you should write about what you know. But what if I don't know anything about... anything?

- What kind of projects do clients want?
- Speaking of clients, how do I get some? (I'm going to show you three excellent ways I've gotten great clients.)
- What about details like... getting paid?
- What's it really going to take to make this work?

If that's what you need to know to get your start, game on! Or, as my son says, "This pleases me greatly."

So how about we start now?

# Chapter 1:

## So, What IS This Business?

> *Ch-ch-ch-ch-changes*
> *Turn and face the strange*
> *Ch-ch-changes*
> **David Bowie**

You might have noticed that this is the third edition of my first book. It was time for an update.

Not because the info in the prior versions had gotten out of date—although some of my tactics for getting work have changed, and I'll share them with you.

Not just because in my first go-round, I mistakenly thought most of my readers would be like me, stay-at-home moms. Turned out about half of you guys are… guys! And you weren't in it for a little mad money; you (like me) went on to support entire families with your writing income. Some of my early readers now travel the world and send me videos from exotic places.

Not because the opportunity to build a thriving writing business has shrunk, because if anything, there's even higher demand today than back in 2005 when I started.

Not even because seeing my old book drove me nuts, between the hideous cover I'd created and the fact my name changed a couple of years ago. (By the way, while life's roads sure can be twisty and bumpy sometimes, it's never too late to create something new that works beautifully).

Nope.

It was time to update the book because the opportunity is so great for you, right now. The freelance writing business has evolved and expanded along with the Internet to the point where every single business you encounter not only needs professional writing services, most of them also now know it.

## There are more freelance writers out there than ever before... and that's good.

See, the demand is still greater than the supply (at least when you take quality into consideration), and there are more writing clients out there than there are writers to help them.

Businesses, whether they sell to consumers or to other businesses, know they face a daunting set of tasks:
- Stimulate demand for their products and services.
- Differentiate themselves from their competitors.
- Tell their story in a way that resonates with their market.
- Nurture leads, helping prospects know, like, and trust them.
- Provide ongoing value to buyers, staying in touch to stay at the forefront of customers' minds in order to build loyalty and promote word-of-mouth advertising.

It takes a lot of words to accomplish all of those tasks. That's a lot of writing—in most cases, more than any one writer could ever hope to produce.

## What kind of writing?

You can sort the writing tasks into two main categories: content and copy. There's some overlap, but most writers are better at one than the other.

## Content is mostly informative.

It educates prospects, builds credibility for the business, and establishes the kind of relationship that makes buyers feel confident they'll get a valuable, effective solution for their problem—and be treated well along the way. Content helps prospects educate themselves before buying, at their own pace and in their own time. It helps them feel safe, sure they aren't going to regret trusting the business they're about to buy from.

**Copy is promotional.**

It grabs prospects' attention then pushes on their pain points enough to help nudge them to the point of making a decision. It makes a bold promise of benefits, backed by facts. It is persuasive, and when it's done really well, hypnotic. It induces sort of a buying trance for prospects, helping them justify the purchase they're about to make.

We're going to focus primarily on content in this book because that's what I know best. If you want to learn copywriting, you should check out courses from American Writers and Artists, Inc. (AWAI). The principles for growing a writing business are the same, whether you're better suited for writing content or copy.

## B2B and B2C

So, we've got content and copy. There's also another way to categorize the writing you'll do as a freelancer: Business-to-Business (B2B) and Business-to-Consumer (B2C). B2B is one business selling to another business. An example would be an accounting software company selling its programs to other businesses. B2C is a business that sells direct to consumers, such as a catering company selling its services to people who are planning parties.

Whether you write B2B or B2C, your goal is to communicate in a way that's effective with your target market. You'll have to write to the right audience, using the words they use, connecting with them so they get the reassurance they need to move closer to the point of buying.

Both B2B and B2C businesses use what we call sales funnels. Funnels work by attracting lots of potential buyers, then taking them step-by-step to the point where some of them make a buying decision. You might write for an audience that's at the top of the funnel, just beginning to explore their options for solving a problem. You might write for the middle of the funnel, where they're getting more serious about studying up on their options. You might write for the bottom of the funnel, where they're on the verge of buying. You might even write for an audience of existing customers, helping your client provide enough ongoing value to keep them coming back for more.

## Why would a business hire freelancers?

Some businesses keep a stable of writers in-house. However, that's becoming less and less common. We're not worried about that kind of business—or the ones that don't think they need professional writing services. There's enough work out there that we don't need to twist arms to get clients.

Look for clients who get it. They understand the need for well-written content and copy. They're practically lined up and waiting for you to write for them. They have a nearly endless list of projects for you, are eager to build an ongoing relationship with you, and want to pay you well because what you write helps them make more money.

## Really?

Oh, yes. Obviously, your revenue is going to reflect the effort you put in, the service you provide, the expertise you develop, and the value of what you deliver. But there is a LOT of money to be made in freelance business writing.

There are all sorts of clients out there for you, ranging from solopreneurs to mom-and-pop shops to small- and mid-sized businesses, and even huge multinational corporations. They all need writing. It's just a matter of finding clients who need what you can provide and who will pay the prices you set... gladly.

There's no shortage of great clients. There is, however, a shortage of great content writers and copywriters. (There are lots of crappy clients and writers out there, of course.) The trick is finding just the few clients you need to make your nut—and delivering outstanding writing that helps them become more successful.

What's possible, income-wise? Write your own check. It all depends on the kinds of writing projects you do and the clients you serve. You could easily make six figures and up (wayyyy up)—if you work for it. You've got to do the do.

Your income will build as you go. When I first started, I hit $5,000 a month within about six months. And that was on a job board, which, as you'll see in an upcoming chapter, doesn't exactly have a reputation for being a fast path to cash.

If you come from a corporate background and feel comfortable swimming in that size pond, you can make VERY good money right from the start. If you're breaking out in hives at the thought of playing at that level, don't worry; you can work up to it. And even if you only ever serve small businesses, you can make a sweet income with only a few clients.

## But not EVERYONE is a good client for you.

This is important to understand. To put it simply, every business out there needs you, but not every business is a good match for you. Success requires eliminating the bad matches—and the faster, the better.

What's a bad match? Either the prospect's needs don't match what you're selling, or they don't have the money (or the willingness to part with it!) to buy what you're selling, or they need what you're selling but not urgently enough to buy, or they need it now and are ready to pay but don't have the authority to make the buying decision.

Your goal is to find clients who need what you're selling, need it now, have the money to pay your fee (without you pulling teeth), and have the power to pull the trigger.

As you build your business, you'll find a lot of businesses that WANT you to write for them but are missing one or more of these qualifications. If you end up working for them, it'll be miserable. However, it'll probably never reach the point where you actually work for them—even though you may spend months chasing them, negotiating with them, and jumping through hoops to win their business.

One of the most important lessons you can walk away with is this: There are more than enough ideal clients out there for you. Your job is to sort through the crowd until you find them.

**Your ideal clients are waiting.**

These are the clients you'll enjoy working with. They'll pay you what your work is worth, on time. They're pleasant to interact with and always treat you with the same respect you give them. They value your mind rather than seeing you as commodity. Build long-term working relationships with this kind of client, and you'll create a business that's a pleasure to own.

Next up, we're going to demolish one of the biggest obstacles new writers face. Keep reading because by the end of the next chapter, you're going to realize how perfectly situated you are to launch your writing business... *right now.*

# Chapter 2:

## Put What You Know to Work—Even If You Don't Know Much

> *The only true wisdom is in knowing you know nothing.*
> **Socrates**

**First, the niche question**

You'll be about three minutes into your new life as a freelance writer before you hear someone tell you, "You need a niche."

And they're right. Kind of. Well, eventually.

A niche is basically a specialty, an industry, or type of project where you've got a lot of experience. This is great if you're coming out of a long career in a certain field, and you want to focus on writing for that field. It's also great if you've got extensive experience creating a particular type of copy or content—say, print ads, textbooks, or press releases.

Why are you getting this advice? A few reasons:

- Because, just like in the medical field, you'll make more money if you have a specialty than by being a generalist.
- Because the faster and better you write, the more money you'll make—and you can write faster and better about topics you already know well.

- Because you can reuse what you learn for multiple client projects rather than wasting time learning stuff you'll only use once.
- Because you can become an expert in your niche, which almost automatically guarantees you'll make more money.
- Because you may even become known as THE writer for your niche, which means you'll be in higher demand and ultimately able to charge higher fees.

Maybe you've got a niche already! In that case, you may find yourself in nearly immediate high demand in that niche. You know it backward and forward, can explain complicated concepts to laypeople, and understand the mindset of your client's prospects so well that you can connect with them easily, right from the start. Those are the telltale signs you've got a niche—and you'd be nuts not to jump on it as you start your freelance writing business.

But wait. What if you don't have a niche? Are you screwed?

Nah. Join the club. Most writers don't start off with a niche. In fact, many get started with writing because they haven't found their niche yet. They've got a string of jobs or careers that just never quite worked—and certainly not well enough to qualify them as experts.

What usually happens—and it happened to me, too—is that your niche will eventually find you. Sometimes a few niches, in fact.

You'll write for one client in a certain industry. Then you'll run into another business in that same industry that's interested in hiring you for a project. Then maybe they'll tell someone else in that industry (not a competitor) about you, and you'll get a call from them. Next thing you know, you've ghostwritten half a dozen books about how to pick up women (yeah), or a couple dozen packages of website text for air conditioning and heating contractors (yeah), or monthly blog posts for marketing companies. It just happens!

Not only will industry niches land at your feet, you'll find the same thing happens with types of writing projects. When I started out, I wrote whatever came my way: sales letters, books, blog posts, product descriptions, website copy, press releases, and more. If a client could describe and pay for the project, I'd do it.

Eventually, I figured out that some projects were super easy for me to write, and others felt like pulling my own teeth out with pliers. Some paid well for the time they took, and others took so long that my effective hourly rate amounted to pocket change.

My firm specializes in ten different types of content projects. We rarely do copywriting projects, and when we do, it's just because an existing client asked for it. In fact, of the ten we do most, we really only do three or four project types on a very regular basis. We've done so many of these few projects that it's been easy to create systems to make the process efficient and profitable.

Even though it's been great developing a few industry niches, what's been even better is developing project specialties. The process for doing these projects is the same no matter what industry the client is in, so there's never the feeling that we're reinventing the wheel. The particulars of the content differ but not the process for getting the information or writing about it.

Either way, though, if you don't have a niche when you're starting out, one (or more) will find you after you've been in business a while. Don't sweat it.

## What if you really don't know anything about your client's industry?

That's going to happen a lot, especially at first. Odds are you don't know a whole lot about the industries any of your initial clients will hire you to write about—at least not from the inside. That's actually a selling point, though.

One of the first clients I had sold car insurance. I've never sold car insurance. I don't understand the acronyms, jargon, or certifications of the insurance industry. I don't like thinking about car insurance. I don't like paying for mine. But I shop for car insurance, carry a policy, and have even used it a couple of times in my driving history.

I am a car insurance consumer. My client's target market is... car insurance consumers. I am them! I can write to them because I am them. That's what my client needed—not an insurance insider who'd be good at communicating with other insurance industry people. The last thing your clients need is a writer who's going to bore, confuse, and alienate their prospects by writing on an insider level.

Customers don't want to have to work hard to get the information they need to make buying decisions. They don't want to wade through a swamp of jargon and complicated insider lingo—they just want to get the information they need in a way that's easy to understand.

Your smart clients will get this: If you can make me understand why you're great, I can write so your prospects understand, too.

You may not be an expert in your client's industry, but you're probably a pretty close match to your client's ideal customer.

This is obviously true for B2C writing, because chances are you've had enough life experience to understand the mind of the prospective customer. Either you've bought what your client is selling, or you've bought something similar enough to understand the point of view of the prospect.

Same with B2B writing. Take any random B2B product or service—say, records management consulting. You'd never buy that as a consumer. It's a service companies use to ensure their document storage practices comply with the law.

You've probably never had to give that a thought, right? But you DO have some of the same experiences a prospective buyer of records management consulting has. You know what it's like to lose something important, what a pain it is to have to pay attention to laws that seem ridiculously complicated, what it's like to shop for something you'd rather not buy, what goes through your head as you evaluate options, and what questions you'd have before plunking down a sizeable chunk of change.

Even though the prospects you're writing to might be sitting in the corner office of a corporation's headquarters, they're still people. Their brains work the same way, and they go through the same buying process any other human would go through. They have a problem that needs solving; they look for a solution; they evaluate the solutions they find; they make the decision to buy; they gather more information to support that decision; then they buy.

That's the biggest shocker I discovered in writing B2B content—it still boils down to people selling to people. I'm people... so I can do this!

## But you can't just make stuff up, can you?

No. You also can't fake your way through a project by being vague. At least not twice for the same client.

For example, once I was working with a new writer who'd approached me about writing for my team. He was still in college and wanted to build a freelance writing business before he graduated. Cool, I thought. So I gave him a test project—a short blog post for an air conditioning company.

Horrible. It was clear this guy had never owned or rented a home, had never paid a utility bill, and had never run a thermostat. He tried to spin the piece in a direction he was more familiar with, but it didn't work. He tried to stretch his wording to meet the measly 250-word count minimum for the test, but it was obvious. And painful. Don't do that.

## So how do you write about an unfamiliar topic?

There are a couple of ways to do this. First, you can interview a subject matter expert (SME) who's involved with the project. Your client may be the SME, or the SME may be someone your client can let you interview to get the information you need. Sometimes the best person to interview is in the client's sales department. Sometimes, it's a customer service rep. You'll get better at figuring out who to interview as you get more experience.

One way I've come up with to make sure I interview the right person is to ask my client who in the company is most passionate about this product or service. This works well for me because I'm a sucker for passion. If you can make me fall in love with your product or service, if you can get me to see the important role it plays in making a business (or someone's life) better, I can turn around and communicate that to your prospects. In fact, I'll probably start telling other people about your product or service even off the clock. Enthusiasm is contagious, and if you can make it come through in your writing, your clients will get even better results from the pieces you write for them.

Second best is doing online research to learn enough to write for your client. There are so many articles, blog posts, and books out there on any topic you can imagine that it's not hard to write well after you spend a couple of hours doing research. Online research is second best because essentially, you're just rehashing what someone else has written, putting their thoughts into your words. It's still valuable content, and to be honest, that's a lot of what my firm does. The value for the client comes in having lots of high-quality content assets written in a way their customers enjoy consuming. It's not groundbreaking, cutting edge information—it's more about building the connection and providing the basic information a prospect needs to make a buying decision.

## Encourage your own sense of curiosity.

Every great writer has a nearly insatiable desire to learn. We are curious people (yeah, in both senses of the word) who love to read, who want to understand how stuff works, and who find pleasure in acquiring new information.

Only a fool dares to play Trivial Pursuit with a freelance writer. We have vast mental storerooms of mostly useless knowledge. Our knowledge base is an inch deep and a mile wide. We love to read—both for the information we gather and for the sheer pleasure of experiencing how words are combined to share ideas.

As a writer, you'll launch yourself on a never-ending quest to improve your wordsmithing skills. You'll discover and develop your own voice, then learn how to use it to make any topic come alive. You'll find yourself writing pieces so good you read them over and over just because they please you (even better when it turns out that they accomplish their goal).

It's all a learning process. You'll learn your niche. You'll master the process of learning and then communicating what you've learned to someone else. We all start from somewhere, and you may be starting somewhere well ahead of square one. Even if you don't realize it, you've been gathering what you need to know all along.

Next up, an introduction to the projects your clients are most likely to want you to write for them. You may be surprised how many of these you could write already… and how fast you could get started earning.

# Chapter 3:

## Clients Want to Pay Me to Write WHAT?

> *You can have any color, as long as it's black.*
> **Henry Ford**

There's a nearly endless list of writing projects clients will pay you to write. I'm thinking you probably don't want to read a nearly endless list, though. Right?

Plus, like we just talked about, there are benefits to specializing in a few project types rather than trying to produce every possible kind of copy or content. You'll get better and faster at these sorts of projects, and you'll make more money at the same time.

A couple of years ago, I decided my firm would focus on ten primary kinds of content. If a client wants something that's not on this list, tough.

Just kidding. Kind of.

We do other content projects that aren't on this list, but they're either too hard to explain briefly or too niched to hold up as an example, because you're not likely to land projects like them.

Point being, you'll naturally gravitate toward the set of projects your clients order most often, and that's a good start on a niche.

Here is our top ten:

1. Website Content
2. Blogging
3. Press Releases
4. Newsletters
5. Ebooks and Special Reports
6. Email Marketing Messages
7. Articles
8. Video Scripts
9. Case Studies
10. White Papers

They're projects you're likely to run into, so let's take a quick look at them. We're not going to get into the how-tos here—although you can get in-depth training on these projects in my Freelance Writers Bootcamp. An overview will do it for now.

## Website Content

What we're talking about on this project is words appearing on a web page. If the content is written right, it'll attract the attention of search engines and increase the likelihood your client's website will show up when prospective customers go looking for the products and services your client sells.

Website content should be written in a way that's persuasive, engaging, and SEO-friendly. The goal is to meet the needs of human readers and search engines alike. Businesses will hire you to write their website content because they know good content will help them get more website visitors and nudge those visitors to take action.

Every website owner needs professionally written content, and not just once. Most businesses recognize the need for a little refresh on their content every now and then.

## Blogging

Blogging can help your clients rank higher in the search engines, which makes it easier for their prospects to find them—even if they don't know the company's name. While website content is considered static content (meaning, it pretty much stays the same once it's published), blog posts add fresh, new content to the site on a regular basis. This fresh content helps lure Google back to the site and ultimately helps Google determine that the site is worth including on its list of search engine results.

Mind you, blogging is not a silver bullet for delivering traffic to your client's site. There's a lot that goes into search engine results page placement, and we don't even know exactly what Google's looking for in the top placements. However, it sure can't hurt if it's done well. Wonderful side benefits include adding girth to your client's site, engaging prospects with information that's valuable to them, maintaining the appearance that your client has a thriving business, and increasing the perception that your client is an expert with information to share.

There's one major reason your clients will pay you to provide blogging services for them. Keeping a blog updated is a total pain in the butt. Blogs are only effective if they are maintained and updated regularly. Given the option of having someone else do this for them, many business owners will recognize the time and money savings outsourcing this task represents.

## Press Releases

Over the years, it's hit me that press releases are rather misunderstood. Lots of people confuse them with bids to get local media coverage. Truth is, as far as traditional media goes, the odds of your press release leading to a newspaper article, TV spot, radio interview, or anything even close to that are slim.

That's not the point. There are two primary reasons for issuing press releases: promotion and protection. The point of the promotional press release is to get good exposure for your client—online and *possibly* in local media. Press releases also help build a hedge of protection around your client's online reputation by ensuring the first results that come up in a search for your client's name are positive.

Clients will hire you to write press releases because they don't know how to do them right, they can't find a news angle, and they're too busy to do it themselves.

## Newsletters

Businesses use newsletters to connect, teach, and sell. It's a mindshare tactic—stay on the forefront of customers' and prospects' minds, and they're more likely to be loyal. Offer specials, be personable, and share really valuable information, and you'll cement your client's position as "my [whatever your client does]" in readers' minds.

The whole point of having a newsletter is to maintain regular contact with subscribers. This means publishing at least once a quarter, but more likely once or twice a month. Whether the newsletter goes out internally to a company's employees to build a sense of teamwork and keep them informed about industry news, out to consumers to provide a mix of relevant content and promotional material, or out to members of a nonprofit organization to keep them informed about events, fundraising, and news, compiling this publication on a regular basis is a lot of work.

Newsletters are such an effective way to maintain contact with people and to boost ongoing revenue that they are well worth the investment they require. Smart business owners recognize the wisdom of outsourcing this task, and who better to help them than you, their writer?

## Ebooks and Special Reports

This project goes by several names, but basically, it is a substantial piece of content that provides valuable information to readers, ultimately giving them enough education about a product, service, or topic to get them to take the next step you want them to take.

The biggest benefit from ebooks is that they build credibility while moving prospects closer to the point of sale by providing the information they need to make a buying decision.

Clients will hire you to write special reports for them to give away at tradeshow booths, any time they give a speech or presentation, to send to their existing customers (with a recommendation that they pass it along to their contacts who'd benefit from the information), and of course, to help put prospects into their sales funnel by offering it free on their website (in exchange for the prospect's email address). Which leads us to...

## Email Marketing Messages

Email marketing is a form of permission marketing. By subscribing to a company's email list, usually in exchange for being able to download a free ebook or report, customers and prospects give permission to be contacted on a regular basis to get information and offers that may be valuable to them. It's an excellent example of drip marketing, where rather than flooding prospects with a fire-hose volume of information all at once, you lead them step-by-step into your sales funnel.

Email marketing is one of the cheapest ways any business can create a steady flow of revenue—either from online or in-office sales. With no printing costs and no postage, it's easy to stay in regular contact with customers and prospects. Most marketing wisdom says you need to "touch" your customers about thirteen times a year in order to stay in the forefront of their minds. There's no easier way to do this, or to automate the process, than by using email marketing

The biggest benefit of email marketing is that it is an automated yet customized way a business can "touch" customers and prospects and drive sales. Because most business owners are extremely busy working in and on their businesses, handling every aspect from bookkeeping to customer service, being able to outsource a task like this—and have it create revenue—is an easy decision.

## Articles

Article marketing covers a spectrum from writing articles and manually submitting them to just a few sites, like EzineArticles, to writing what would be considered feature articles—extremely high quality, like those in a trade journal or popular publication.

When people have a question, a need, or a problem, they go online to find answers and solutions. Sometimes these are very personal, pressing, painful issues. Other times, the searcher is a lot more casual. Either way, when they go searching, it's with a pretty high level of skepticism. They're hoping they'll find good information but halfway expecting they'll end up sorting through a bunch of ads, taking their chances on a solution that might turn out to be the online equivalent of snake oil.

If they stumble onto articles that meet them where they are, provide good information, and lead them to a solution that looks realistically promising, there's a virtual relationship created that's going to benefit everyone involved.

Even though anyone anywhere can get articles published online, high-quality articles are a sure way to build a perception of expertise. Imagine if you go looking online for information on a topic and you find several useful, credible articles on someone's website. It'll begin to look like this website is the absolute authority on that topic. You'll appreciate the information you get, begin to trust the site owner, and be open to hearing any other information you can get there.

## Video Scripts

The world of online marketing is slowly changing. While the power of the written word used to reign supreme online, the advent of online video has made video marketing all the more important.

Every video needs a script. Video scripts are documents specifically crafted to be read aloud. They can be read by a presenter on camera or as a voiceover on a video presentation. Videos are used to pre-sell a market on an idea, to teach how to do a specific task, to answer questions from the market, and for a variety of other purposes. Anything that can be covered in articles or blog posts can be covered in videos.

Depending on the client's needs, you may also need to suggest images or other visuals that show as the script is read. This ranges anywhere from a photo to an infographic or even a sort of animated theme, just a phrase-worth of text at a time.

Video marketing is sweeping through all aspects of Internet marketing. From independent Internet marketing professionals to corporations, you can find many prospects for this service. Many local businesses are catching on to the idea that online videos are a good marketing tool. The only problem is that most of them don't realize that the words in their videos have to be well written. Those who do get it will hire you for ongoing video scripting projects—and pay you well for your help.

## Case Studies

A case study is sort of like a testimonial on steroids. It's a bit like a special report dedicated solely to how a product or service made a significant, measurable difference for a specific person facing a substantial challenge. It's the equivalent of having your most satisfied customers line up to personally visit each of your prospects and share their success stories over coffee.

There's a reason the case study is the darling of marketing firms everywhere: Social proof sells. In a marketplace filled with skeptics, nobody wants to be the first one in the buyer pool. We all want Mikey to taste the cereal first.

Case studies are pretty involved projects. They involve interviews, research, and a deep understanding of the client's sales process. They pay very, very well.

## White Papers

White papers are used by most businesses as a way to give their potential business clients education and information on a particular topic. They help business buyers make decisions about the products and services they need.

White papers act as a report or guide. They not only inform and educate business decision makers, but they persuade the audience of a specific point of view or solution. They are more than simple brochures. Whitepapers carry more authority than a regular report or a marketing publication. They are informative, well researched, and engaging and can be used to introduce specific ways of thought, new technology, innovation, and other products. You'll need to strategize, interview, outline, write, and maybe even arrange for design for the white paper. With all that's involved, they also pay very well.

That's just a taste of the variety of projects clients will pay you to write. You could easily make a very nice income focusing on just one type of project, or you could shake it up by learning how to write several kinds of content. They all take practice, but it's easy to apply what you learn doing one project to the next project you do.

Now that you have an idea of the kinds of projects clients will pay you to write, let's take a look at a few ways to get clients.

# Chapter 4:

## The Best and Worst Way to Get Started

> *There's nothing in this world so sweet as love.*
> *And next to love the sweetest thing is hate.*
> **Henry Wadsworth Longfellow**

If you want to start your freelance writing business with training wheels, like I did, you might consider registering with a job board. There are lots out there, but the biggies are Guru.com, Elance.com, Fiverr.com, and Odesk.com. With some variations, they work the same way: Clients who need something written post projects for writers to bid on.

**When I was starting out, I loved those sites. Now that I know how to get clients on my own, I rather hate them. Weird.**

It used to be a great way to start if you did it the right way. It can still work for you, but there are easier and faster ways to start making more money than putting yourself in what could very quickly become the race to the bottom of the fee scale.

While Guru was my mainstay for the first years of my business, at this point I can't even remember the last time I logged on. My firm generates a lot of referral leads and has ongoing clients who've been with me for years. Many of my clients have clients of their own that we write for—we have forged a working partnership where we provide all sorts of content these end-user clients need. My clients get to be the one-stop shop, their clients get what they need, and we stay busy. Very busy!

However, if I were starting out, I would still look at the job boards as an option—even if I never got a single project there. One reason is that it's a good way to see what clients want and how they describe what they want, and good practice in pulling together a proposal and figuring out what to charge. Even if you never land a gig there, you'd still benefit from that kind of practice.

The other reason—and this one's kind of freaky—is that it's one of the fastest ways to summon projects from out of the clear, blue sky. It's like, by bidding on a project, some sort of message is sent out into the ether announcing that you've got availability... and nearly every single time I've done that, a project has plopped into my lap. Think maybe the universe rewards taking action?

Now, like I said, I'm going to show you some much more direct ways of landing much better clients in a bit. What I'll show you has the potential for bigger checks, long-term arrangements, and better projects.

However, you may have reasons of your own for wanting to start with job boards, and I get that. No judgment here. When I first started, the idea of talking to a business owner was horrifying. I didn't know what I was doing, and even though I was certain I could figure it out and produce what they needed, I was terrified of looking like an idiot in a conversation. I also worked bizarre hours sometimes and couldn't schedule business meetings or even phone calls with clients. For me, with those factors and my periodic hermitness (I know, not a word!), the job boards were ideal. Even though there was more money to be made elsewhere, there were other benefits that made this a better choice for me at the time.

Maybe that's your story, too. While I hope you'll go after better projects and clients rather than wading through dozens of bad gigs on the boards to reach the few that are good, that's no reason not to tell you how I got good results on the boards. 'Nuff said, right?

## Here are my tips for getting your first clients from job boards.

### Pay a buck! (or several)

If you go with the free level of membership, you're in competition with tons of writers—and writers who are (how can I say this nicely?) cheap.

What does this mean for you? If you're competing against writers who are desperate, they'll underbid you. They're the ones who'll write someone's biography for $50. Frankly, you don't want to compete with them on price. And the type of client you'll get is not what you want.

If you join at the lowest level of paid membership, the herd thins considerably. You're not making a huge investment, but you'll set yourself apart.

For about $30 a month, you'll be on a whole different level. It's almost a guarantee that you'll make the fee back in the very first project you do. Most of the people listing projects open them only to paying members—it's kind of a litmus test for them. So you'll find better projects and less competition for them.

### Work on your profile page.

When you don't have any feedback yet, this is all your potential clients have to go on about you. Make it look good. If possible, link to writing samples or at least offer them. As you get projects, remember to update your information.

Take a look at other writers' profiles and follow their example. But don't copy them. That shouldn't even have to be said, right? But running my own profile through Copyscape revealed several freelance writers who'd copied and pasted mine into theirs—and only a few bothered to change some telling details. Why a freelance writer couldn't write a unique profile is a mystery to me, but all I'll say is, "Don't do that."

## Choose a pay range that makes sense.

Most of these sites offer you several choices. Think long and hard about your hourly rate. Remember how important perception is, too. Would you expect better results from a $7 haircut or a $70 one?

I've learned a lot about setting an hourly rate. When I started with Guru, I set my rate at $28 per hour. Not quite sure why—it just seemed reasonable. But my hourly rate goal back then was actually $75—quite a difference. I thought nobody would hire me at that rate. Wrong! But it took a while to get the nerve to raise my rate.

In the meantime, I got really busy with projects, got better at bidding, and improved my skills and systems. Never gave another thought to the hourly rate posted on my info page. Then I got a gig from a client who wanted to pay my hourly rate for some editing. Now that's awkward. "Um, yeah, about the $28 per hour—it's really $75." I did the project and immediately updated the hourly rate on my profile.

I wondered what would happen. Would the projects suddenly dry up? Would my bidding success rate crash and burn? Or would this change somehow make me more appealing to writing clients?

Actually, nothing really happened. No measurable change in the success rate for my bids. Nothing dramatic at all. But, it came in very handy after getting gigs. A few times clients asked for more work on an hourly basis. And long term, this strategy paid off by pre-qualifying my prospects. It's a different client who wants a high-quality writer than the one who just wants to pay the lowest fee possible.

You'd think the next time I bumped my posted hourly rate, I'd do it without internal drama. You must be new here.

It came time to raise it to $100. Gulp. Surely, nobody would want me at that rate. I feared my business would circle the drain and never recover. Certain disaster, right?

No. Not even close. People want the high-priced expert. They know it'll cost them more, and they don't care. They want it done right. It's more of a hassle to hire someone cheap, have to spell out in excruciating detail what they want done, then fix it because something went wrong than to just pay to get it done right in the first place.

## Create excellent bidding templates.

They are a huge time saver and make bidding easier. Don't send them as-is; customize each one according to the project's particulars.

Tweak them. Test them. See which variations get you the most response. You want your bidding process to be as easy as possible. If the site offers a sample template, use it. But reword it!

This is how you make your first impression on these prospective clients. Proofread it. Read it out loud. Make it perfect.

## Get to know the flow of the site.

You'll find that many of your clients are new to the site, too— you'll make them feel a lot more comfortable if you can lead them through the process. It's not complicated; it's just new.

Create a flow chart to help yourself visualize what happens after you're awarded a project. Who does what next? You want to know this process cold before you're in it for real.

## Get busy bidding.

You should set a bidding goal for each workday. I recommend five bids a day, five days a week. Bid on projects first thing when you start working. At first, it could take a while as you get used to the flow of the site. You'll have to sift through the projects to find some you're confident you can do.

It's a good idea to start with about five different types of gigs you'll focus on at first. For example, you could specialize in blog posts, website content, email messages, ebooks, and press releases. Look for these first and place your bids. Then go back and look at the other projects to see if there's anything interesting.

**Do your best.**

On all of these sites, there's a built-in feedback system. Your feedback is like gold—protect it at all costs. Go the extra mile by beating the deadline, turning in excellent work, and being as courteous as an angel (even when you feel like you'd like to fit your client for a pretty pair of cement shoes).

You want nothing but perfect ratings. If you get anything less, make sure you pay attention to what went wrong and fix it next time.

You'll choose better projects with practice, but you need to be prepared for the occasional dog. These are the projects that take longer than you expected, where the client wasn't clear, or where you had to do more revisions than you'd like.

Take it in stride. Be a complete professional. Get your payment and good feedback and learn from your mistakes.

**Ask for referrals.**

This works for clients you get online and locally. Once you've done a great job for them, ask if they know anyone else who might need your services. They'll be happy to pass your name along (unless they want to keep you all to themselves, which happens!). This way, you can really get a lot of mileage out of your marketing. One project could turn into a few projects in the blink of an eye.

Always be sure to thank anyone who gives you a referral that turns into business. If it's someone local, I always try to send a bottle of wine or some other goodie—or at least a handwritten note. It's a little more complicated with online clients because you don't always have their personal contact information, but be sure to thank them.

**Follow up with your happy clients.**

You do a project for a client. They're happy. They pay. You go back to looking for work, starting from square one—right?

Wrong! If someone hires you to write, chances are, you'll be needed again.

Sometimes it's been a while between projects. Sometimes they forget they'd really like to work with you again. Sometimes a year or more passes between gigs for that client. But you can solve that easily by staying in touch. Every month or so, if you haven't done anything for a particular client, send a little email. You could even do a monthly newsletter to send to your clients, and build your connection with them that way.

If you email them, your message doesn't need to be anything fancy or high-pressured. Just a little "Hi—just touching base to see how you're doing with your business. If I can help you with anything, just let me know." It's that easy.

Follow-up is a foundational principle of doing business. You should be in touch with your clients several times a year. If you stumble onto an article that would interest or help one of your clients, forward it with a little note.

Again, while these bidding sites are WAY better than "content mills" (websites where you can get paid pennies to write articles in the hopes they get enough readers to make you a few bucks), they're nowhere near as good as the other options I'm going to show you. They're not quite the bottom of the barrel, but they're close. Your individual circumstances may make job boards an appealing option, though.

The benefits are that if you use the site's payment system, you're virtually guaranteed to get your money, you'll get a good education about what clients want and how they ask for it, you'll get practice at preparing proposals and marketing your service on a regular basis, and you may even get some great projects and clients.

Up next, we're taking a major leap forward on the client quality scale. You're about to discover a gold mine of writing projects that you can land with minimal time spent marketing.

# Chapter 5:

## Become the Secret Sauce

> *I'll keep you my dirty little secret.*
> **All American Rejects**

What could be better than a steady stream of work, virtually guaranteed payment, and very little ongoing marketing? Actually, there are two things, but we'll get to them in the next two chapters.

Writing for agencies is a giant leap forward from trolling for work on job boards. You'll make more money, spend less time looking for work, and practically forget how to chase your paycheck. Once you connect with an agency or two where you're a great fit, it's possible to eventually take on as many projects as you'd like to—often regularly recurring projects that you become really good at writing (which means you also get faster at writing them, which sends your effective hourly rate through the roof over time).

There are a few different kinds of agencies we'll cover in a sec, but they all have a few bits in common:

- They do all the marketing, sales, proposals, invoicing, and customer service.
- They are always looking for great writers to add to the team. Sometimes they've got more work than writers;

other times they've got more writers than work. It can take a while to become one of the top-shelf writers, but once you do, the arrangement will work as long as you keep producing top-notch writing.

- They pay you directly. The classy ones guarantee you'll get paid, even if they run into a payment issue with their client.
- They treat you as an independent contractor, not an employee.
- They don't give a rip when or where you do your work… as long as you deliver the good stuff, on time.
- They make money on every word you write.

## Agencyception

(Hey, writer's prerogative to make words up when needed. Shakespeare did it. Saw that on the Internet, so it must be true.)

I have an agency. My agency works for agencies. See it now?

Some of the best clients I ever landed on Guru worked at agencies that were looking to beef up their teams by first testing out some hired hands they rounded up on job boards. After the initial projects we did together, we took the relationship to the next level—working together directly. They were so glad to have a writer they could trust for excellent, on-time content that left them some margin for profit (maybe even a lot of margin), and it soon became a relationship that was hugely profitable for everyone involved.

Of course, it didn't take long for me to end up exhausted.

As a solo freelance writer, you'll face a capacity issue at some point. You can only write so much, and when you reach the point where you can't take on any more work, you're at capacity. You'll probably try to take more on anyway because you don't want to disappoint your client… which will most likely end with your client being disappointed because you're late with work or your work quality starts to slide.

Yeah, that sucks. When you get an email from a long-time client asking what happened, it may be the same not-so-subtle nudge that led me to start an agency.

I'm not going to get into the logistics of building a writing agency in this book, but if there's interest, I'll do a separate book on it. The learning curve is sharp and deadly, and I'll tell you right up front that there have been white-knuckle times when it seemed I was inches away from losing it all. But once you iron out the kinks, it can be a very sweet and profitable business model.

Anyhow, I've seen how this works from both sides of the table, so I can give you the full story. Check it out to see whether this is a fit for you.

### What are these agencies you speak of?

There are three basic kinds I've worked with: marketing agencies, web design firms, and Internet marketing or publishing companies. They have one thing in common: They need words. A lot of words.

They've got projects lined up that stand to make them a sweet bundle of cash, and the only piece remaining before they can launch is that they need stuff written. Could be website content, press releases, blog posts, course materials, product descriptions, special reports… or a host of different projects.

They don't make money by spending their time writing—they make it by selling products and services. They make more by outsourcing to freelancers and tacking a profit margin onto the top of what they pay these writers.

### How much could you make writing for an agency?

Less than you'd make if you had direct clients of your own. A lot less, in fact. But still, you can make some very good money writing for agencies.

In most cases, your agency client will ask you for pricing on a particular type of job. They may already have a budget for that project, and if your price fits, they may hire you. Sometimes they'll contact you earlier on to get your price, then tack on a markup of anywhere from 50-300% to present to their client.

Yeah, you read that number correctly. Trust me on this—you never want to know what your agency client charges for the work you did. Set your prices at a level that makes you happy and then mind your own business. You don't know all the factors that go into the final price to the end user. Chances are, they've got a long list of expenses that you don't have, and that profit covers them. Nobody's in business to break even or take a loss, and your writing deliverables are a product your client is reselling at a profit. That's capitalism, folks, and there's no more beautiful system anywhere. (If this idea bothers you, you may want to stop and read *Atlas Shrugged* and then come back in three months when you're done to keep reading this.)

Economic debate aside, did you catch that bit about YOU setting your own prices? That's a pretty great benefit of working with agencies. You need to set them at a level where they can profit by reselling your services—but you still get to write your own check.

That's the other thing—your check. In most cases (and certainly with my own agency), as long as you deliver quality and make your deadlines, you'll get paid. It's up to the agency to chase the check, not you. My agency has only been stiffed a few times over the years, mostly because I've figured out how to make sure that doesn't happen—but when it did happen, I paid my writers from my own pocket. It hurt. A lot. But it was the right thing to do.

## Why should you work for website developers?

This is one of the biggest goldmines I've found for landing writing projects. Typically, business owners hire a firm to make their website for them. They specify colors, graphics, how many pages, and what these pages should cover.

But they rarely provide any content!

These poor techies are left with nothing when it comes time to put words on the site. They ask, beg, and plead with their clients to please send some text. The client usually responds with something like, "Oh, just write something."

Yikes!

The techies go into panic mode and try to crank out some words. It's a matter of left-brain, right-brain, I think. They're geniuses when it comes to meta this, and source that, but words may not be their forte.

The client ends up with a gorgeous site that reads like garbage.

Their prospects take one look and click onto the next company's site. It's a complete waste of money for a company to buy a website and fill it with bad writing. The techies know this and are more than happy to outsource the content creation to freelancers. They can tell their clients that their text will be provided by a professional writer, you get a lot of steady work, and everyone wins!

Plus, now more than ever, business owners understand the importance of doing things the way Google wants them done. This means high-quality, relevant content that has just the right frequency of keywords in it. It's not something just anyone can sit down and whip out—there are established best practices now that need to be followed if there's any hope of winning love (and website traffic) from the Big G. Google has also started showing massive preference to websites that feature frequently updated content (sounds like a blog to me!), which means even higher demand for well-trained and talented writers who can get this never-ending task handled for business owners.

Take this a step further and you may never have to market again. Website developers and marketing consultants are the source of most of my firm's work at this point.

## What about Internet Marketers?

You can usually find these folks online or at conventions and seminars. They're building monetized websites, selling products or how-to information products.

One of the primary ways they get traffic is through article marketing and blogging. People read an article online, follow the link in the resource box, and find a whole site devoted to some specific niche. It could be about beekeeping, kitchen utensils, narcolepsy—you name it, and there's a site about it.

One goal they have is to create an authority site—a site that's so rich with information (BLOG!) that's useful and valuable to their visitors that people (and Google) start to consider it the go-to site on that topic.

They also know how hard it is to pry people's contact information from them, and typically produce a slew of special reports they can dangle as an ethical bribe to compel prospects to surrender the booty. You find a site that offers the solution to your problem, you see they offer a free report that looks like it'll help, and you're happy to trade your email address to get access to that irresistible information. What follows is a set of email marketing messages aimed at nudging you to take action (buy something!).

Voila! Prospect has now entered the sales funnel—the next step in converting traffic to paying customers. Who do you think writes all these reports? Sometimes these Internet marketers can write and want to spend their time writing—but usually not. Much of the training they get from their gurus stresses the importance of outsourcing tasks like writing. Many are entrepreneurs who understand they will make more money by building businesses than by working in those businesses.

They're always searching for good writers. The name of the game for Internet marketing is quality content promoted with effective copy.

## Garbage Means Good News!

Much of what's out there is absolute garbage, which is good news for freelance writers. There's no shortage of work! Most of these projects don't even require much in the way of research.

If you build a working relationship with one of these marketers, chances are that they'll keep you very busy. In fact, they become a little territorial about their writers. (Does nice things for your ego and your bank account!) They appreciate the value of a good writer and are hesitant even to share your name with a colleague. If they share you, you might get too busy to write for them.

Many times when I've worked for Internet marketers, the working relationship has grown to the point where I not only wrote blogs or articles but became one of their primary (or only) content creators. For several of them, every time they want to create a new product, I get a call or email about a nice, juicy project accompanied by a sweet check. Most of the time, content creation for a course involves watching videos they create and writing a book or a study guide to go with the videos.

Everything you create for your Internet marketer clients must make them money. It may be used in their sales process (like the special report), in driving traffic to their websites (articles, press releases, video scripts), or as part of their actual product (ebooks, courses, print books). So, while they're not technically agencies, the idea is the same—and so is the potential for getting all the projects you need to make your nut.

## How to Become an Agency's MVP

- Always deliver high-quality work. Work your butt off to make sure what you send is the best it can be.

- Hire a proofreader to minimize the risk of delivering text that has typos or grammatical goofs. It's easy to become blind to what you've written. Fresh eyes will catch your errors—better to have those eyes be in the head of your proofreader than your client.

- Deliver on time or die trying. OK, that might be extreme, but there's a lot to be said for delivering ahead of the deadline rather than making your client poke you for an update.

- Run your text through Copyscape... just in case. I've had pieces of content that I wrote from my own head ding in Copyscape—sometimes bringing up other pieces I wrote! It's worth the 5¢ per search to buy confidence that your work won't trigger duplicate content issues, even by accident.

- Don't pester your agency clients. They either have work for you or they don't. Touching base now and then is fine, but don't cross the line into hounding them.
- Don't keep asking for pay increases on ongoing projects. Unless you're delivering more value than what was contracted for originally, chances are good that the answer is no. You can always try, but you also have to understand that the agency's only got so much margin to mess with (like with my agency, there's no 300% markup for sure!).
- Be cool with being anonymous. You probably won't have contact with the client—and getting a byline is even less likely.

I've got some writers on my team who've been with me for nearly a decade, and they get dibs on every new project that comes in. My firm has served some agency clients for about that long, too, and we are the only team of writers they use.

How do you make that happen? The first one's the hardest. After that, if you've done a great job, your agency clients will refer you to others (as long as you can still help them first). They'll also bring new clients onboard, which means more projects for you.

But that first one...

In the next chapter, we're going to look at some strategies for landing ideal clients. These tactics will work for landing agencies. The important bit to remember is that you've got to present yourself in terms the agency will appreciate, namely that outsourcing to you will be a hassle-free and fantastically profitable venture.

# Chapter 6:

## Direct is Delicious

> *We say who, we say when, we say how much.*
> **Pretty Woman**

Want to make a lot more money? Want more control over your projects overall? Then it's time to jump in and swim with the big boys. You can do this by landing clients directly—no job board, no agency, no middleman of any kind—just you and your client.

When you start working directly for clients—either B2B or B2C—the potential earnings (and potential challenges) take a sharp upturn. Nobody's taking a cut; what you charge and collect is what you keep (well, after taxes). Also, nobody's marketing *for* you, nobody's covering in case a client decides not to pay, and nobody but you is holding your client's hand.

Here's where you build a wildly lucrative business—once you get the kinks worked out. The hurdles you'll face are easy to fix by designing systems in your business, and the rewards are far greater than you'd experience with other types of clients.

Specifically, you're going to have to handle your own marketing, pricing, and billing. You're flying without a net here. You screw up, and it's on you—you succeed, and the booty's all yours.

For some writers, it makes sense to just dive right into working with direct clients. If you've already got a list of businesses you know would love to hire you to write for them, you should GO FOR IT. NOW. This is definitely you if you've just hung your freelancer shingle after a career that's given you a solid education, hands-on experience, and a list of industry contacts who wouldn't even think about questioning your ability to write for them.

For others, you might feel like you need the running start you get from working with an agency (or even a job board) first. Get a bunch of great portfolio pieces and some experience, and you'll grow confident enough to go after your own clients.

For still others, maybe working for clients directly is a great idea for another time in your life—when you've got the bandwidth, confidence, and financial strength and stability to go for it. The need for freelance writers has become so great that you can make a very nice income no matter which route you take, so don't worry if you feel like this one's more than you want to take on at this point.

## What Makes Them Want to Work Directly with YOU?

Direct clients, just like any other kind, go looking for freelance writers because they don't want to take content creation on as an in-house task. Some businesses have huge marketing departments (with big, juicy budgets) and detailed specifications and systems for getting the content they need, and they prefer to work directly with freelancers rather than with an agency. Some businesses don't have the huge budget or super-defined systems for describing what they want but still prefer to work directly with a freelancer.

Direct clients realize they'll get a level of attention and dedication they could only get from working with the same writer for an extended span of time. There's no extended learning curve for the writer. There comes a point where the writer is able to anticipate the client's needs without having to spend time working out details. There's not as much back and forth needed to gain clarity. They know they can just call the writer and say something like, "Remember that thing you did for that project? We want another one like that, but this time with these details," and it'll make sense!

They probably also realize they'll get more bang for less buck by cutting out the agency middleman. They also figure that working one-on-one directly with a freelancer is the closest they can get to having an in-house writer without having to pay benefits.

Think about these benefits, this concierge-like level of service, and how hassle-free an arrangement like this will be for your direct clients. When you market to them, focus on these benefits, and you'll be singing their song.

## They're Everywhere… But How Do You Reach Them?

So, how do you find these direct clients? Here are just three ways I've found some of my best clients. Try them out and let me know what works for you.

## One: Your Friends and Family List

This is so simple. Just send an email out to your friends, family, neighbors, and acquaintances saying you've just started your freelance writing business. Ask if they'd take just a minute to think about anyone they know who owns a successful business— someone they'd feel comfortable introducing you to either by email or in person. If you'd like to focus on a particular business type, that's even easier: "Would you introduce me to your accountant?"

You might also want to include a little something to sweeten the pot and make it easier for your contacts to approach their contacts with this introduction. Maybe say you'll write a free press release for the business, kind of a no-obligation taste of what you can do for them. This makes it easier for your contacts to feel like they're helping you AND their business-owner friends.

It's easiest if you set up a spreadsheet, list all your contacts, and keep a record of when you emailed them. You don't have to do them all at once—and be sure to add a little personal touch to each message rather than just sending an impersonal email blast out to everyone in your contact list. Don't send them as a group—send each message separately.

## Two: Direct and Drippy (but in a good way)

We're talking direct response marketing here, campaign style. You can learn more from Dan Kennedy, Gary Bencivenga, Jay Abraham, Perry Marshall, Joe Sugarman, and other famous direct mail masters than I can teach you. They've all got books and courses that are well worth the investment. I'm still learning this craft, but I'll show you the basics here, and even the basics may be enough to get you started.

Identify a list of potentially ideal clients, make them an irresistible offer, then follow up until they die or buy. This plan follows the best practices of direct mail—and no matter what detractors say, it works. It's a proven strategy-based, step-by-step process for marketing that puts the law of large numbers to work for you. The more you do it, the better you'll get and the more clients you'll land. As a bonus, you'll be able to do the same for your clients.

1. **Create your list of prospects.** There are a thousand ways to do this. Don't get hung up on this step! You can buy a list, scrape a list from existing lists, or even pay a virtual assistant to put a list together for you.

2. **Send a postcard or other introductory piece.** Catch their attention and make an offer they'd be crazy to pass up: high value, no risk to them. Maybe you want to offer a free copy of your book (I do this, but you have to have a book first), or a webinar, consult, or special report. Tell them how to take advantage of your offer (and make sure it's a way that you'll be able to track, so you know what's working for you).

3. **Follow up.** You might need to send several offers over a period of time. You might want to try different pieces: postcards, letters, lumpy mail. It can take multiple touches before a prospect responds. Plan for this, rather than

getting all depressed when you get no response from your first attempt!

4. **Do it again, and again, and again.** Once you crack the code and create a campaign that helps you land a few clients, don't stop! You always want to market enough to build your business to twice the size you NEED it to be. This will enable you to be pickier about the projects, clients, and rates you get for your business. Also, by having twice as many clients and prospects in the pipeline than you actually need to make your nut, you'll experience more peace and confidence (conducive to more success!) than if you show up in life looking like a desperate freak.

A solid direct response strategy is like a water spigot—turn it on, off, up, and down as much as you want, and you'll develop the superhuman power of being able to grow your business at will.

## Three: Get Out there and Press the Flesh

In-person networking can work wonders for your business. Either that or it'll make you throw up on your shoes. As an introvert, this took some practice for me. In fact, while I was sitting in my car psyching myself up to walk into the first networking meeting I attended, I promised myself I could leave after having at least a two-minute conversation with five people. I didn't stay a second longer than that, and just thinking about how awkward it felt still makes me want to puke.

But it gets easier. It's a good kind of pain because it's important to learn how to connect with other humans. Writers can easily become total hermits, but that's not necessarily a lifestyle that's going to max out on satisfaction. If you're curmudgeonly or shy, if you're far wittier and more charming in writing than in person (me!), if you'd just as soon chew your own arm off than go make small talk, you can still make a fantastic living as a writer. So don't freak out just yet—you can actually reach a point where this becomes pleasant.

You'll hear mixed reviews about joining the Chamber of Commerce or other official networking groups. They can be a great source of work as you're starting out, if you do it right. It'll cost you, but you should designate part of your revenue to use for marketing expenses. A Chamber membership will probably cost $300—$500 per year.

On top of that, you'll probably need to pay for networking lunches and breakfasts. So it's not the cheapest way to go. But it can pay for itself with a good project pretty quickly.

A couple of tips:

## Go to each event with a killer introduction speech.

Usually you get about a minute to introduce yourself. If you can't wow them with what you say, you're wasting your time and money. You just bought yourself one heck of an expensive scrambled egg breakfast.

Make sure your intro stands out as being creative, professional, funny (if possible), and loud enough that everyone hears you. Most people just get up and say the same old stuff, and nobody's really listening. If you can get up and make a positive impression, you'll be amazed who'll come talk to you afterward. Here are two introductions I've used that had people lined up to get my card:

At a women's networking luncheon, I went up front with a pillow stuffed under my shirt so I looked pregnant. I said, "Sometimes you've got big news that sort of announces itself." I pulled the pillow out and said, "Other times, maybe you need a press release. I'm Sue Anderson, owner of Triumph Communications, where choice words help your business succeed."

At another luncheon, I went up front, hid my eyes with my arms, and said, "One... two... skip a few... ninety-nine... a hundred! Ready or not, here I come!" Then I looked around, and said, "Hide and seek's a blast when you're seven years old. When you're trying to market your business, it's not so great. If you could use a little help boosting your company's visibility, give me a call."

The key is to be interesting without being too weird. Use props. Shake it up a little. Make sure to bring something fresh each time you go so that people look forward to your spiel.

Lots of people there have no idea what a freelance writer is or does, so you may have to do some educating over the months you're involved. Take it slow and just pick one type of project at a time.

Don't go with the goal of making a virtual ticker tape parade of your business cards. It's better to chat with a few people and really listen to them than to get with everyone in the room for three seconds each. See whether there's anything you can do to help them with their business or life (recommend a plumber, an accountant, a free advertising venue). Do what you can to be relevant to them. You'll feel most empowered at these events when you become sort of an unofficial host, a connector. Introduce the people you meet to others you've met there and help them find what they need.

**Bring a door prize.**

Offer a free something writing-related (not a discount coupon!)—it's an easy way to give something that's impressive, useful, and serves as a good foot in the door for potential new business. A free press release is a great idea.

Dress it up by making it a gift certificate that's presented beautifully, maybe in a mug filled with candies or attached to a nice bottle of wine. With your prize, include your business card (duh!), and include the value of the prize on its description.

You'll get extra exposure when your prize is announced, a nice opportunity to sort of audition for a potentially regular client, and—worst-case scenario—you get something to add to your portfolio.

The great thing about working with direct clients is that you don't need so many of them. If you're building your business on the job boards, you're going to need dozens of clients each month to make good money. If you work for an agency, you won't need so many (and you won't have to look for clients once you're in the stable). But if you work for direct clients, you can easily make your nut while working for only a handful of clients.

So, we've covered boards, agencies, and direct clients. What could be even better? How about working with NO clients at all? That's up next, so keep reading.

# Chapter 7:

## Look Mom, No Clients!

> *I love humanity... but I hate humans.*
> **Albert Einstein**

I'm going to be straight with you here. I LOVE my clients. Some I've had for close to ten years. They've hung in there with me when my business went through growing pains, they've offered words of encouragement and support when life got messy, and they've valued what I deliver enough to enable me to support myself and my family for close to a decade.

But there are times I'd FAR rather magically be able to make money writing without clients. I imagine what it would be like to forget the meaning of the word *deadline*, to write only about topics that interest me, to dive head-first into a work schedule that's as all-or-nothing as I'd like it to be, binge writing sessions followed by a few days off.

Fairy tale, right?

Not at all. I've gotten a taste of what's possible and suspect that with some significant shifts, I could turn this into reality within a couple of years.

It's all about passive (or passive-ish) income, and it's a money machine every freelance writer should get busy building. Basically, you write about topics you love, then generate income over time from work you did once. You have complete creative control, write on your own schedule, let the big marketing guys do the heavy lifting, and then do a little happy dance each month when you get paid.

There are many, many ways to do this, and I'm always learning and experimenting with what works best. Some ways require you to have an extensive reservoir of knowledge about your topic. Others only require that you have a strong curiosity and passion for the topic. You don't have to have a *New York Times* bestseller to do this, and you don't have to pack your garage with a mountain of books you hope to sell. You don't even have to be picked up by a publisher. This is an income stream you could build starting right now!

We'd be looking at another book to cover this angle of writing thoroughly—maybe I'll write it, if there's interest. But for now, it's enough to plant this little seed in your mind… at some point you want to write and publish as your own client, getting paid in perpetuity for work you do now.

High level here, just three ways you could become your own client and make a sweet passive income from your writing:

- **Write and publish Kindle books.** Could be fiction or non-fiction, long or short. Do a top-notch job of writing, get a stellar cover, and publish. Then collect royalties month after month. There's an audience out there for almost any topic you could imagine, and you'll have the power of Amazon behind you, marketing *for* you.

- **Longer book? Get it in print, too.** There are many print-on-demand publishers out there, and one is owned by Amazon (Create Space). You can get your book in print and never have to order more than a single copy (not even required, but you'd be a dork not to buy your own book just to see it!). Again, it'll sell on Amazon. Maybe not a blockbuster, but any amount it makes as recurring income is pretty sweet.

- **Blog your heart out.** There are LOTS of excellent courses (see Ryan Deiss or Jeff Walker in particular) about building a blog that makes money. You can make money by recommending products to your audience, selling ad space, or even creating your own course or marketing your book through your blog.

I've seen this work—in big ways and small—for too many writers not to tell you about it! One writer I know wrote a series of short erotica books to help make ends meet. (Not touching that. Or that.) Once she learned the publishing process, she realized her income was only limited by how much she could write. Another got together with a group of girlfriends and published a cookbook series that made a small royalty income month after month.

Other writers I know now have about a 50/50 split between income from client work and income from their own publishing. One is still getting royalty payments from a book he wrote thirty years ago!

Not a bad thing, getting paid long term for work you already did!

I wish we could go into this topic in more detail, but I just want you to think about it and start writing on the side for now. Meanwhile, let's keep going to cover some important odds and ends that'll help your business grow big and strong enough that you can support yourself while you write these other projects.

# Chapter 8:

## Nuts and Bolts

> *It's the little details that are vital. Little things make big things happen.*
> **John Wooden**

There are lots of bits and pieces you need to know. You could figure it out on your own over time, but if I can help you shave a lot of aggravation off of your learning curve and help you make more money, faster, I'm happy to do it.

Probably the easiest way to cover these odds and ends is with a question and answer format. Ready?

### Question: How Do You Set Your Prices?

If there's one question freelancers have on their minds, it's this: How much should I charge?

It's a good question.

Charge too little and you're practically working for free—and you're left wondering whether that 9-5 job might be a better deal after all. Charge too much and you might not get any work.

So, what do you say when a prospect asks the dreaded question, "How much would you charge for..."?

Pricing's kind of a big hill to climb. We'll take it in small steps.

The first thing you've got to decide is your hourly rate. Not too many clients will ask about it, although I have a few who have.

Typically, the best situation to run an hourly tab is when you're doing work that's bordering on consulting. For example, I once had a client who always had great ideas buzzing through her head. She'd ask me to spend some time brainstorming how she could market a new site or product. She knew my hourly rate was $100, and I billed her in increments of 15 minutes. We'd worked together enough that I billed her monthly, knowing she'd pay.

Even though your hourly rate will work well sometimes, it's almost always better—for everyone—to bill a flat fee.

Why? Think about it.

If you get paid $10 per hour to rake leaves, your employer will wonder whether you're working as quickly as possible, or if you're dogging it.

But, if you estimate it'll take five hours and charge a flat fee of $50 to rake the leaves in one yard, they'll feel better, knowing just what to expect.

Now here's the beauty part—what if you become such an efficient leaf raker that you manage to do that same yard in only three hours?

You've given yourself a raise! Your ingenuity is rewarded. And your employer is still happy because you kept your end of the deal.

Same deal with writing.

Why would a client hire you without knowing how much the project will cost in the end? And why would you want your income tied to your time? It's always better to get paid on results rather than for your time.

But your hourly rate is good to know even when you're charging a flat rate for a project. Especially when you're just starting out, it's a great way to back into your fees for projects you do often.

Now, if you're working for an agency, you're not setting the prices. You're looking at what's offered and taking it or leaving it. You still need to know your target effective hourly rate, but that's for your own use as you decide whether to take a project.

It's crucial to understand that pricing is an experimental process. You'll suck at it before you get good at it. You'll find yourself working for free (or in the hole!) now and then. You'll get better with practice.

There are two ways you can go about pricing your services. One *seems* easy, and the other, sadly, involves math.

## First, the easy-ish one.

Find out what other writers are charging for projects and use their pricing to help you make your own. The trouble is that you can't know whether your background, experience, and skills match theirs—or whether their prospects go for those prices, or even whether they're truly charging those prices. Many writers post their prices online, but many don't. I use other writers' prices as a sanity check once I've come up with my own pricing. If I'm way off, there's some element I haven't considered.

## And now the math one. Blech.

You'll need to come up with your desired effective hourly rate, apply it to a solid estimate of the time involved in writing the project, then adjust for intangibles.

1. What do you need or want to take home each month as a salary?
2. What do you need to add to that figure to cover stuff like savings, insurance, and taxes? Add it in.
3. What do you want to add in to cover marketing expenses, training and education, equipment and software, or anything else that you'd count as an operating expense? Pile it on.
4. How many hours a month will you work? This includes everything: marketing, client follow-up, writing, proofing, revisions, billing, the whole guacamole.
5. Divide your target money amount by your hours.

This is your target effective hourly rate. Let's say it comes to $100.

Next, you'll have to figure out how long it takes to complete various projects. Let's say 30 hours for a white paper. We're looking at a starting point for white papers of $3,000. Now, you may be faster, so you'll make a higher hourly rate. Or, you may be slower, in which case you'll want to get faster! You may be exceptionally knowledgeable on the topic or develop astonishing skills that deliver a high return on your client's investment, in which case, you should charge more.

It's a crapshoot at first. Don't stress out about your prices; just vow to get better at pricing the same way you work to get better at writing.

One way you'll get better at pricing is by tracking your work. You'll need a timer for this. Keep track of how long it takes you to do things:

- How many minutes to write an article?
- How long to do research?
- How long on the phone with clients?
- How fast do you write 500 words? 1000 words?
- How long to proofread?

So, work with what you can figure out easily and go from there. Don't be afraid of making mistakes—just learn from them. There's no scarcity of projects to work on as you perfect your pricing.

If you blow your pricing by going too high, you'll have another chance on another project. If you blow it by pricing too low, you'll work like a dog for a while and learn a great lesson for the next time.

The idea is to keep good records and analyze them often. You should also do this on a bigger scale to see how much progress you're making toward your monthly and annual goals. Whatever you pay attention to grows—so pay a lot of attention to your profitability! Spend some time weekly, monthly, quarterly, and annually to set and track goals.

- What do you expect to do this month/quarter/year?

- How many new clients?
- How many of a certain project type?
- How's it going?
- What's working well for you?
- What's not working so well?
- What can you tweak so you do better next month?
- Where did you waste time?
- What was easy?
- What was most profitable?

Spending this time strategizing does wonderful things for your business. It helps you direct your efforts toward the most profitable writing projects. It helps you see how close you're coming to your goals. And it helps you grow your business in an orderly way rather than running in every direction at once, chasing after dollars like a lion after the slowest antelope in the pack.

## Question: How Do I Get Paid?

This is really two questions: How does the money reach me? And, how do I make sure I get paid?

Get thee to PayPal. Everyone uses PayPal. PayPal will take a small bite out of every payment, but it's fast and easy for everyone involved. It's simple to use, but it does take a few days to get activated. Start on it first so you can get paid quickly when the time comes. Checks work nicely from ongoing clients, but PayPal's faster and easier.

Getting paid? That's rather important, isn't it? After all, it's kind of the whole point of running a business. There's a little risk in getting screwed, but not much. I've been stiffed only three times, and every single time, it's been because I bypassed my own money rules, general common sense, and the little voice screaming, "NOOOOOO!"

Part of the anti-stiffing protection is being selective about your client list and setting your prices high enough to weed out the tire-kicking thieves who'll take your work and run. You can always go to Small Claims Court, but who's got the time? Try to prevent the problem from the start. Use a standard contract, and get a deposit.

Nearly every project I do now requires payment in full, up front. I figure that in many ways, what I'm providing is a product—and people pay in advance for products. My clients know they'll get great work, and they also know I have a team of writers I need to pay. My writers are happy because they know they'll get paid, and whenever possible, I pay within a day or two of when they invoice me, rather than making them wait 30 days or so.

### Question: What about Health Insurance?

Don't get me started. Unless you've got some other way to get coverage (spouse?), you're on your own. It's going to be costly. You'll need to work with a broker who can provide legit options. Don't fall for the Internet ads that promise massive discounts with some stupid-low priced membership card. Get real insurance.

Life insurance, too, since we're talking about it. Oh, and your retirement fund. See, you're on your own. You have to be a grown-up and take care of yourself. You don't have an employer doing this for you.

### Question: What about Taxes?

Seriously? You want to go there, too? I've come to terms with my annual godawful tax bill by realizing this: I made money. Now I owe.

Get an accountant who understands freelancing. You'll have to decide which tax entity is best for your situation (i.e. sole proprietor, LLC, Corp., etc.). It varies depending on where you live. Do NOT try to do your own taxes. It's a stupid move, and you'll kick yourself if you do it.

### Question: What if You Get a Bad Client?

For those of you just starting out, I hear you: "BAD client? I'd be happy to have ANY client!" Well, hang in there, because you'll have your share, too! And if you're prepared in advance, maybe you can flatten the learning curve a bit.

I had one project that I'd love you to learn from. I'd been working on it for a month. It should have taken one week, tops. And it got to the point I felt like I might just puke if I had to look at it again—or if I got another call from this client asking for yet another round of revisions.

Confession: Basically, I want her to pay up and go away happy—but mostly just go away.

It'll happen to you, too.

"Bad" clients give you lots of points to ponder—an opportunity to grow. Run some of these thoughts through your mind:

- How can I turn this into a win for both of us?
- What gut feelings did I ignore as I got myself into this project?
- What about when I know I'm right and my client is wrong?
- What effect will I allow it to have on my business (and my sanity!)?
- How can I choose better next time?
- What tweaks can I make to my systems to make sure this doesn't happen again?

Here's what I do:

First of all, take a moment to be grateful. After all, I HAVE a bad client. That means I've got a client base. It also means most of my clients are good or else this one wouldn't stand out.

Second, take responsibility. I chose this client as much as they chose me. We probably talked at length before starting, and I'm the one who made the decision to move forward. This means I can also choose better next time!

Third, stand by your commitment. I signed a contract and will honor it to the end. While doing this means I might sacrifice some sleep, the fun of working on a "good" project, and even my appetite, at least I don't have to sacrifice my integrity.

Fourth, check out your contract verbiage. I knew there was a phrase I should include, but I never got around to it because it had never been an issue before. It reads something like this: "The writing fee includes X rounds of revisions within 30 days." With these eleven words, the whole problem could have been avoided.

Fifth, about being "right": Yes, I wrote some absolutely killer copy—the first go-round. Yes, to be honest, after all the revisions and client input, I think it's now less than stellar. Yes, I'm the copywriter and she's not. But, she's the client, and my goal is to serve rather than to be right.

Hey, "bad" clients happen. It should be no surprise. The only question that remains is how you'll deal with it. Will you allow it to derail your business, life, and mood? Or will you redeem the situation, create value in it, and learn to make better choices next time?

## Question: How Do You Save and Back Up Your Work?

Pay attention to how you set up your documents file. I recommend creating the following files to start with:

- a file for each client
- a sub-file for each project
- a file for your portfolio
- a file for your invoices
- a file for proposals

Now, about backing up… I hope you'll never see the screen of death that says your computer just crashed, because it's stress nobody needs. Obviously, you should save your work often. But as a backup, use an offsite backup, and I would consider buying an external drive, too.

Carbonite offers a free backup system that I use and recommend. You can customize it to back up the files you want, as often as you want. Very cool. The idea is that if something were to happen, you can go into the site and download all your goodies again. Sure beats having a coronary! I've used several similar services through the years, but this one's the best I've tried. I can access documents from my account via my smartphone and can even email them that way.

An external hard drive has proven to be a lifesaver for me now that I'm on my third laptop since I started my business. The old one ground to a halt gradually, which gave me the opportunity to make sure I had every document backed up that I wanted to keep. I can keep all the old stuff on the external drive and just plug it in to access those files when needed. It's overkill, kind of like wearing a belt and suspenders, but I'd rather know my documents are safe and accessible than have that moment of agony when you realize they're gone.

## Question: Do I Need a Website for My Business?

I used to say a website was just a nicety but not a necessity. Going to bump that a bit toward the top of the list of needs now, however. Even if you build a simple site that can house your portfolio and provide a way for a prospect to check you out and contact you, it'll be helpful. It used to be that website construction was a total pain in the neck, requiring specialized programs, coding, and a big bottle of Advil. Now with the WordPress platform, it's much easier. You can learn nearly everything you need to know to build a simple site by watching YouTube videos, too.

Buy a domain name (I currently use GoDaddy) and a small hosting package (Host Gator has one for about $5 a month). Install WordPress and build your site. It'll take a while to get it like you want it to look, so don't put off finding client work until you're done. You could also pay someone to build your site for you, of course! But if you learn to build WordPress sites, it'll give you more control over your own site and the ability to build and work with sites for your clients.

Those are the most frequently asked questions, and I hope they were helpful to you. While it would have been great knowing these tidbits before building my business, learning them in the process worked, too. Next up, we're going to talk about your next steps.

# Chapter 9:

## Let's Wrap It Up

> *When you dance, your purpose is not to get to a certain place on the floor.*
> *It's to enjoy each step along the way.*
> **Wayne Dyer**

By this point, you've either decided freelance writing is not for you—or that it seems like the perfect fit for your life.

Freelance writing gives you a way to work when and where you want, to work on projects that are interesting, to earn fees you set, and to work for clients you like—all while doing something that comes pretty naturally to you.

It's just a matter of getting going.

So, how do you get started? How do you go from wistful wishes about someday becoming a writer to actually getting paid for your words?

**If you're building a writing business from nothing, I want you to picture the path ahead as a train track.**

The left track is what you'll do to get clients; the right is developing your services. If you've already got clients or you already know how to write the projects your clients want, you've got a head start. Either way, as you make progress on one track, you need to also work on the other track. You'll probably find that as you get clients, your skills improve because you'll learn how to write what they want just in time to write for them. And as you learn how to write different writing projects, you may find that clients appear out of nowhere who want you to write that project for them.

**Make a plan and then stay the course.**

I'll warn you—now that the idea of becoming a freelance writer has settled into your mind and got you feeling excited about the business you could create, you're going to run up against all sorts of distractions. From shiny object syndrome to outright sabotage, you will encounter multiple opportunities to bail on this dream.

Your own mind may whisper mean stuff to you about how you really *can't* do this, how it's too late and all the good clients are taken, how you just aren't smart enough or brave enough or organized enough to make it work. (We all get that now and then!) You may even hear crap like that from the people around you. (That's a discussion for another time.) And for sure, you'll probably be approached by someone with the "business opportunity of a lifetime" along about the time you commit to building a writing business. (Run!)

Don't fall for it! You can do this. It won't happen apart from your own effort, and it means learning, working, experimenting, and practicing, but the journey is actually pretty cool if you'll take those first steps to get going.

**How can I help you build your own writing business?**

Hopefully this book has filled your mind with all kinds of great ideas and enough how-tos that you can take your first steps. It's just a start, though.

My best advice is this: Get your hands on other freelance writers' books. Listen to podcasts (Ed Gandia's in particular—there has not been a single episode that hasn't been fantastically helpful). Attend seminars and courses that teach the skills you want to learn. Work with a coach when you've got the resources to do so. There's a ton of information you can find online—both paid and free. The best plan is to find a teacher you really resonate with and learn all you can as you get started.

If you want more training from me, I've got a few resources to offer.

## Get My Working Writer, Happy Writer Home Study Course

www.WorkingWriterHappyWriter.com

In addition to this book (which you've already bought, of course... more on that in a second), this course gives you:

- Step-by-step instructions for creating your own freelance writing website.
- One more client-getting tactic you can use to attract excellent clients.
- A detailed sales funnel plan you can use to identify ideal clients, market your services to them, and keep your project pipeline full.
- A quiz you can take to show you which client-getting tactic is likely to work best for you right now.
- A 30-day plan with action steps to keep you on track and moving forward with your business at a manageable pace.
- All of the organizational documents I use every day:
- A project management dashboard
- A proposal template
- An invoice template
- An editorial calendar
- A reading list of the best books I can recommend as you grow your business and create the life you want to live.
- A downloadable copy of my book about content marketing.
- My guide to creating a winning portfolio that can even make money for you while you build it.
- A sneak peek at one segment of the Freelance Writers Bootcamp.

Now, since you've already shelled out some money for this book, I'd like to give you a price break on the home study course. How does 50% off sound to you? All you have to do is input this promo code: SMARTREADER when you purchase the course, and you'll get a sweet discount.

## Freelance Writers Bootcamp

www.FreelanceWritersBootcamp.com

This Bootcamp was designed for writers who've already gone through the Working Writer, Happy Writer course, to help you learn HOW to do the various projects you'll offer your clients. It's constantly evolving as I add and update more project types, and you get lifetime access, which means you'll never have to pay a cent to get the new information. You'll learn exactly what I do to market, land, price, and do the most common writing projects.

Each project module includes:

- What kind of clients are most likely to hire you for this project, how to find them, what will make you attractive to them, and some ideas on pricing.
- The same process documents I use to train the writers on my team so that we produce consistent, high-quality content for my clients.
- Recommended resources for research and further learning.
- The secret weapons we use to help us create highly engaging content our clients' prospects are eager to read.
- Valuable add-ons you can include to help and delight your clients.

As a Bootcamp member, if you've got a burning question that's keeping you stuck, you can contact me through the Bootcamp portal, and I'll send back a brief answer to get you moving again (as soon as possible—usually within 24 hours).

You'll also get exclusive access to monthly group calls where I'll answer questions submitted by Bootcamp members about writing projects and business building.

Plus, when my writing team expands, I'll look first to my Bootcamp members to see who might be a good fit for a new project. You get paid work, and I get writing help!

## One-On-One Coaching

Some of my students prefer an even more hands-on approach to being mentored. I learned how to make money writing by working with a coach. For me, that was ideal because I'm an eager student, do all my homework without complaining or excuses, and thrive on checking stuff off lists and getting a pat on the back while watching results unfold before my eyes. Every time I've hired a coach, it's been worthwhile. So I get it when people contact me asking for coaching.

The thing is, I am a working writer. I could write day and night and never run out of projects. I followed the model my coach taught me, and it worked like magic. I've built a writing business—brick by brick—and it's changed my life (and the life of the writers on my team).

I adore my family and friends, spending time writing, cooking, hanging with our growing ark of animals (dogs, cats, chickens), traveling, reading... the list is long. So, I've learned to guard my time. That's why I go about my coaching program a little differently than other coaches might—and differently than I used to do it.

Rather than trying to get as many clients as possible, I'm going the opposite way. I believe our time together should be focused, action-intensive, and based on a mutual all-out commitment. That's the only way to help make sure it's as productive as possible so that your writing business pays you back—and more—during our time together. It's expensive, it's limited to just a couple of students a year, and it's by application only after you've gone through the Bootcamp.

However you proceed in your business, I hope this book has been helpful to you. One of the greatest joys in life is creating something useful—and I know you'll feel that each time you create and deliver content for your clients, and especially when you look at the business you've created using your writing talent, your entrepreneurial spirit, and your sweat.

Wishing you a thriving writing business and the satisfaction of knowing you've built something beautiful.

Happy writing!

**Susan**

# Would You Do Me a Favor?

If you've enjoyed reading this book, if it's given you some inspiration and guidance on how to build your own business, I would SO appreciate you leaving a review on Amazon.com. Everyone looks at reviews before deciding whether to buy a book—and the more honest the review, the better.

If you've got constructive criticism, I'd love to hear it so I can improve the book and make it even more helpful. If you wouldn't mind, send it to me directly by email at:

sue@workingwriterhappywriter.com.

Thanks so much! I truly believe freelance writing is a growing business and that there are more than enough clients to keep every good writer well paid and busy. That's why I've shared so openly about what it takes to build a business and why I'm hoping this book will find its way into the hands of every person who's serious about getting into freelance writing, one of the best businesses ever!

# About the Author

Susan Anderson started Triumph Communications in 2005 upon realizing this Internet thing was here to stay and that there sure was a lot of horrid content already clogging it up. She started off as a solo writer, creating so much highly rated content for clients that she rose to the top spot on Guru.

That was enough to build some confidence and credibility, and she decided Triumph should serve more and better clients… and that she couldn't do it alone. Switching to an agency model made bigger wins possible—for the clients and the writers. Of course, now the hitch was finding great writers to add to the team.

Seemed like the next logical step was to create a course to show others who love to write how to get paid for their words. Two birds, one stone! Her *You Write, They Pay* book and course has trained hundreds of freelance writers how to build businesses of their own… and some of those students have become part of the Triumph team in the process.

Even though she's a bit of a hermit, she's enjoyed presenting online and in-person training on freelance writing as part of Eben Pagan's Traffic School and Ignition programs and Coffee Shop Millionaire. She was even flown to Fiji to teach there.

Susan splits her time between Huntsville, Alabama, and the Tri-Cities area of Eastern Tennessee. Mom to two teens and a small ark's worth of animals, she counts walking on fire and breaking a wooden arrow with her throat as piece-of-cake accomplishments in comparison. If she's not writing, she's probably taking a long walk with the love of her life, trying to convince her chickens to weed the garden, or wiping drool off of her 1959 Volkswagen Beetle Ragtop, Miss Mabel (built by said love of her life).

Made in the USA
San Bernardino, CA
06 July 2015